The Joys of a Small Wage

Very drole
on the dole
I'd rather be
a sausage roll
tatty on the outside
tasty on the in
nobody knowing
where you've been
what you've done
or what you've seen
"At bloody work all day!"
is what I'll say
working jolly hard
to bring home my pay
even though it's a pittance
it's enough for my admittance to
the cinema.

Anally Yours

Jenny from Barlow's [Plymouth]
thinks she is right all the time
she talks down to me as if I am dirt
but she must be anally retentive,

And Daryl from Boss [Leighton Buzzard]
always wants it blacker than black
and yesterday at half the price
and maybe he's anally receptive.

No matter where
no matter when
the working world is full of assholes.

Andrew, college boy [Doncaster]
thinks he'll do it by the book
because the book, and he, knows best
so he's definitely anally perceptive

And Judy from Texas [Rochford]
she's got a mouth like a D.I.Y. superstore
an ego to match her flamboyant hair
and she's definitely anally pro-active.

There is no love lost
there is always a cost
my working world is full of assholes.

Lettered Things in Numbered Places

We work in a steel rectangular box
just around the corner
with professional unprofessionals
and Little Jack Horner
the power of unorganised organisations
driven by the meek
lettered things in numbered places
moved around by the weak
rebels and unions slaving side by side
making the work force
still all working for a living
under the rule of the big boss
out on a golf course
voice of opinion falls on deaf ears
of the factory shelves
and like boxes we are lettered things
in numbered places ourselves.

Office Politics

Dumb as a post
that's stuck in the mud
keeping the elite out
and the rabble in
a compound, made from compound
to compound the issue
is a training ground for the squads
of mods and bikers to begin
now ready for the front line
of defence that we find offensive
and willing to take aim
to maim the enemy within
General Confusion gives the orders
and the march to nowhere starts
desk barricades, fax evades
the artillery of hole punch holes
brandishing AK47 staple guns
ready to fire with hairline triggers
and why on earth are we fighting again?
Because none of this figures.

Long Light

I've waited a long time for it this year
it's very late but finally it appeared
I don't even know what it is called
if it has a scientific name
or even if anyone else knows it exists
but I can see it right now.

Late afternoon, late summer
as the sun is slowly drooping
and the sky is silver blue
the light changes and becomes what I now call "long light"
longer shadows, longer nights
and a longing for summer to start all over again
it's all around me now
reflecting off of the sea gulls
casting shadows onto the corrugated aluminium of the industrial units opposite
picking out detail in the wilting leaves of the sycamore by the factory door,

I was getting worried that I'd missed it this year,
or whether because of our unusually late summer
it wouldn't arrive at all
but I hadn't and here it is to cheer me up a bit
whilst all around and everything else
is staying short.

The Magic BUNZL Van

The Magic Bunzl van
don't come no more
with its delectables
and its delicious driver
she fixed the vending machine when it went wrong
and replenished
oh boy, did she replenish
the Lion bars
Boosts
and that look of knowing
when she spied the missing snack
from the front of those twirly dispensers
because someone had rocked the machine
and got free goodies,

It meant nothing to her
she still got paid
but she knew it was a factory where such people worked
and I hope she didn't think that when she looked at me
I know I didn't think that when I looked at her
I thought of replenishment
Lion Bars
Boosts
and I would have rocked her
got some goodies
given her a finger of my Kit-Kat
or a bite of my Twix
but she don't come round no more
and we've got a new machine
and a new replenishment lady
who doesn't do it for me at all.

The Cutest Courier in SS2

There is a parcel in despatch
on the desk by the hatch
and it's for collection,
It's been there a few days
gathering dust becoming grey
waiting for some action,
Then today, Friday
she arrives
in her white unmarked van.
- "Allo, got a parcel to collect,
going to labels supplies."
she reads from her manifest.
I try to digest
what she's asking
without going all stupid like the last time she came.
- "Oh yeah, I know the one
but its got no delivery address."
She says nothing, takes it in her stride
and follows me through the doors to the desk,
and I place the parcel in front of her
nearly at eye level
I don't know how she reaches the pedals
of her Ford Transit
I've seen her driving round town
fast
and slow and stressing
she's passed me on my bicycle
unnoticing
with her blue tooth blue ear.
I've never known what company she works for
she was just a white van woman
but now I can see
its A.N.C....
A Nice Courier
Another Naughty Courier
Ample Naughty Curves
Absolutely No Chance!

She duly peels off the barcode and slaps it on the box
with more dexterity than any other courier I've ever seen
her touch refined over time
all this time, less than a minute
seems like an hour
but never does she crack any hint of mood
her face a stern non-emotive nonplussed defence mechanism
a necessity from dealing with blokes in despatch areas and warehouses all over Essex
she signs the docket
and can't remember the date
which I find strange
because she must have written it a hundred times today
maybe she too has had a moment, a lapse of concentration, a whiling,
but I doubt it.
- "The 7th" I prompt.
She signs her name in the time honoured traditional illegible squiggle
that might begin with a C, or maybe an E
hard to tell, but the most I'll ever know.
- "OK." she says.
- "Thank you." I respond
and as she walks away she looks up at me
and only briefly
affords me a thin, tiny smile
before heading back out the door to her van.
- "Have a nice weekend." I call after her
and she is gone.

Never has a brown cardboard box
brought on so much warmth
(except that time we had a huge bonfire in the back garden).

Windy Day

It's the time for migration
the call of warmer climes
but not many birds will be flying south today
coz it's windy as fuck.

Everything is heading north
clouds, plastic, leaves, cyclists all with ease
blown along by a warm southerly gale
I had to pedal on my way in this morning
but even up hill was a breeze
easy on my knees and calves.

The gulls are trying to use all the skills of sailors
angling themselves and using gravity
to try to make headway towards the sea
but the only direction they head in is sideways.

My boss made a snide remark
about how I put that tarpaulin on, not being up to scratch
but its holding its own today
testament to my cub scout knot-tying days
they weren't in vain
I just hope it don't rain
by the time I have to head home
to Southend.

Crane Fly

I'd forgotten all about that crane fly
that had got trapped in the big tub of swarfega-like
orange hand washing stuff
it had struggled valiantly
but in vain
as the next time I went to wash my hands
its struggle had finished
and there to, its life
a shifts worth of greasy dirty inky hands later
and it had disappeared
sunk, submerged
into a bright orange world of de-greaser, detergent and granules
it must have been attracted to it at first
but how it would have stayed clear if it could see itself now
its sodden lifeless useless body
reappearing at the bottom of the tub a month later
amongst all the filth of a printing factory workers daily chores
to remind me what a cruel, unforgiving world this can be
to add another chapter in this short story
and another page in this book.

Later,
when I returned to the lavvy
to reflect a little more
there was a new tub of swarfega-like orange hand washing stuff
and when I went out to the skip
there it was
the spent, unwanted, used, unloved crane fly corpse
in the spent, unwanted, used, unloved empty tub
amongst the spent, unwanted, used, unloved waste of the factory
waiting to be taken to a place where
all the spent, unwanted, used, unloved things eventually end up,
Pitsea Landfill.

Old Thurston's Finest

Using other people's noses
is better than mine
especially when Colin is around
for there is a bad smell
you are so sure to tell
when his bottom does make a sound.

Lighting the Way

A new card craft and scrap-booking shop has opened up
opposite work now
it is wholesale as well as retail
which means there are more members of public around nowadays
instead of the usual factory workers, van drivers or office staff
there are bored middle aged ladies with a new hobby
grandfathers with too much time on their hands
and families too, who go on shopping outings because they've nothing
better to do with their lives,

- "Daddy, what's that?" mouths the little face staring from the rear
window of the people carrier,
- "It's a forklift truck sweetie" comes the learned reply
which distracts him from his parking and he mounts the kerb
all be it gently,
The heads bob in unison with the suspension
- "That gap is big enough for a 17 ton curtain-sider"
I think to myself
as I proudly drive about the front yard
moving pallets and stillages
pleased with myself for opening a young pair of eyes
all be it briefly
to the joys of a gas powered Nissan 1.8 tonne counterbalance with
sideshift and heated seat.

I go and spoil it all by dropping a pallet of 2017m's
unceremoniously onto the floor
and the face in the window smiles.

Looks Like Snow

- Mornin'.
- Morning.
There's an awkward queue at the coffee machine
- Number 12?
- Yeah.
There's that all too familiar early morning routine.
Same jokes, same remarks, same ice breaker of "the weather"
instead of something better
some of these guys have worked here for more than 15 years so you'd think they'd be able to muster more than the mandatory, obligatory, statutory
utterances and responses that they make every day
week in week out year after year.
- Taken a turn!
- Yep, looks like snow
- Nah, too cold for snow!
- Forecast says snow by Thursday
- Nah, too cold for snow!
- Too cold for snow?
- Yep
- Then how does somewhere like, Finland say, get snow, it's bloomin' freezin' up there!
- Ain't you got no work to do!
- You know there's a bite in the air when the seagulls are coming in land!
- Don't have snow like we used to.
- Was it 63 or 65 when we had that really bad winter?
- 63 I think.
- Nah, 65.
- Couldn't even get out to the coal bunker it was so deep.
- Wasn't it 64?

and so it goes on
morning after morning
the awkward queue at the coffee machine
- Number 12?
- Yeah.
That all too familiar early morning routine.

Dusk (on an Industrial Estate)

This warm summer eve
is blissful would you believe
on Temple Farm Industrial Estate
except for the skivers
and practicing learner drivers
with all their attempts and mistakes.

Guestimate

There's not much that's poetic around here
it is mainly industrial
and come to think of it
there's not much industry,
mainly complaining
putting the world to rights
and backstabbing
the nearest thing to poetry
word play
that I've seen round here
is the word "Guestimate"
it's used more than frequently
in fact some people have based their whole entire career on it
and there is no ounce of poet in them
in fact there is no ounce of worker in them
irony to them, is something the wife does
they use excuses for reasons
and pass the blame
the buck
their life by
and the point.